Yom Kippur
Festivals Around the World

Words in **bold** can be found in the glossary on page 24.

©2017
Book Life
King's Lynn
Norfolk PE30 4LS

ISBN: 978-1-78637-068-6

Written by:
Charlie Ogden

Edited by:
Grace Jones

Designed by:
Matt Rumbelow

A catalogue record for this book
is available from the British Library.

Yom Kippur

Festivals Around the World

Hello, my name is Jacob.

When you see Jacob, he will tell you how to say a word.

What is a Festival?

A festival takes place when people come together to celebrate a special event or time of the year. Some festivals last for only one day and others go on for many months.

Some people celebrate festivals by having a party with their family and friends. Others celebrate by holding special events, performing dances or playing music.

What is Judaism?

Judaism is a **religion** that began around four thousand years ago in the Middle East. Jewish people believe in one God who they pray to in a **synagogue** or a Jewish place of **worship**.

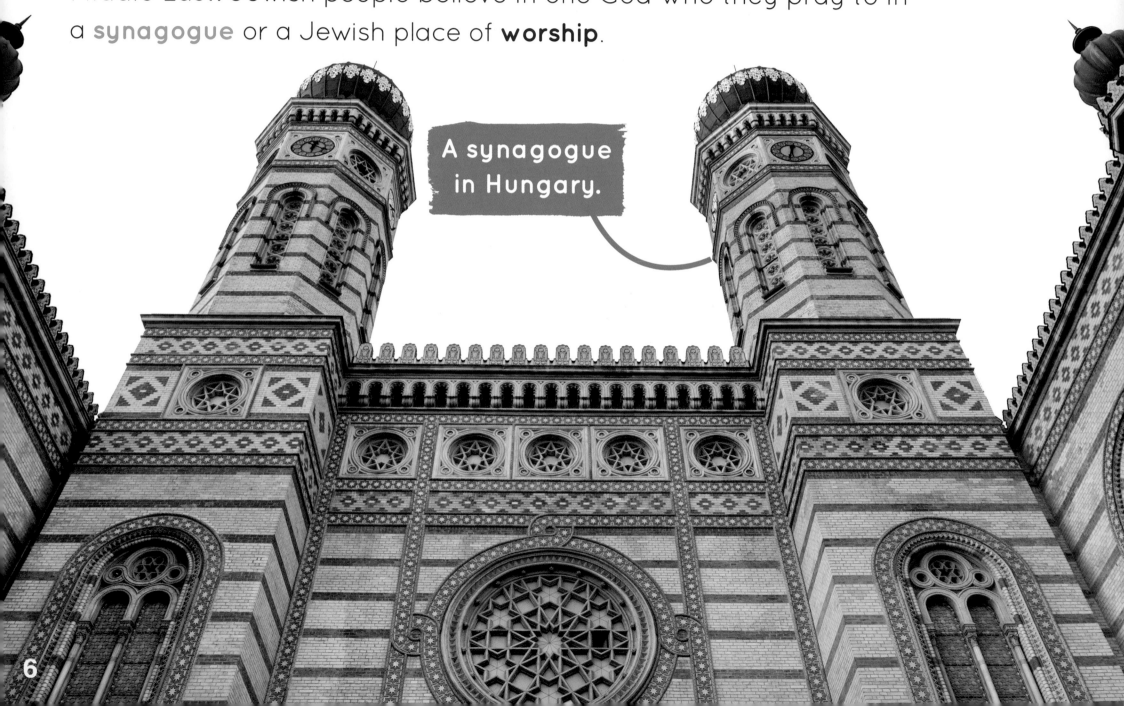

A synagogue in Hungary.

Rabbi

The word rabbi means 'teacher' in Hebrew.

Jacob says:
SIN-A-GOG (Synagogue)
RAB-EYE (Rabbi)

Jewish people read a holy book called the Torah. The Torah sets out God's laws, which instruct people on how to practise their **faith**. A **rabbi** teaches Jewish people about God's word through the Torah.

What is Yom Kippur?

Yom Kippur is a Jewish festival that is celebrated in September or October of each year. On Yom Kippur, God decides what will happen to each Jewish person in the next year.

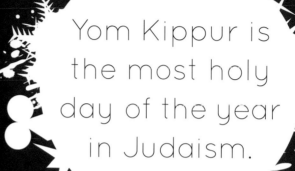

Yom Kippur is the most holy day of the year in Judaism.

Yom Kippur falls on the last day of **Yamim Noraim**, which is a ten-day-long festival when Jewish people make up for the bad things that they have done in the last year.

Jacob says:
YOM KIP-PER (Yom Kippur)
YAM-IM NOR-AIM (Yamim Noraim)

Yom Kippur is also called the 'Day of Atonement.'

The Story
of Yom Kippur

A long, long time ago, there lived a man called Moses. Moses was sent by God to save the Israelites who were being kept as **slaves** in Egypt.

Jacob says:
IS-RAIL-ITES
(Israelites)

Moses led the Israelites to Mount Sinai, which was far away from Egypt. After 40 days at the top of the mountain, God gave Moses two large stones with the Ten Commandments on them. The Ten Commandments are ten important rules that Jewish people must follow.

When Moses brought the stones down the mountain to the Israelites, he saw them worshipping a golden cow. Moses was angry because the Israelites should only have been worshipping God. He got so angry that he broke the stones by dropping them on the floor.

Moses went back up Mount Sinai to get more stones from God. When he came down again, the Israelites were very sorry for what they had done. They made up for what they had done by worshipping God and saying prayers. This was the start of Yom Kippur and now every year Jewish people **atone** for the bad things that they have done.

Eve of Yom Kippur

The day before Yom Kippur is called Erev Yom Kippur or the Eve of Yom Kippur. On Erev Yom Kippur, Jewish people worship God in a synagogue and give to **charity**.

An important part of Erev Yom Kippur is the **kapparot**. The kapparot is when Jewish people swing bags of money over their heads before giving the money to charity.

Sometimes chickens are used in the kapparot.

Jacob says:
CAP-PAH-ROT (Kapparot)

Day of Atonement

On the day of Yom Kippur, Jewish people atone for the bad things that they have done in the last year. They believe that if they atone and worship God, then God will look after them for the next year.

One way that Jewish people atone during Yom Kippur is by not eating or drinking. This is called fasting. Jewish people also do not wash, go to work or drive cars during the festival.

Fasting

Jewish people begin fasting when the sun goes down on Erev Yom Kippur. They can eat and drink again after it gets dark on Yom Kippur.

Before Jewish people start fasting on Erev Yom Kippur, they have a very large meal. At this meal, Jewish people usually eat with their families and wear white clothes.

Prayer and Worship

Jewish people get up early to pray during Yom Kippur. An instrument made out of a ram's horn, called a **shofar**, is played after prayers on Yom Kippur.

Shofar

Jacob says:
SHO-FAR (Shofar)

Jewish people are ususally supposed to pray in a synagogue three times a day. But as Yom Kippur is such an important day, Jewish people are supposed to pray five times.

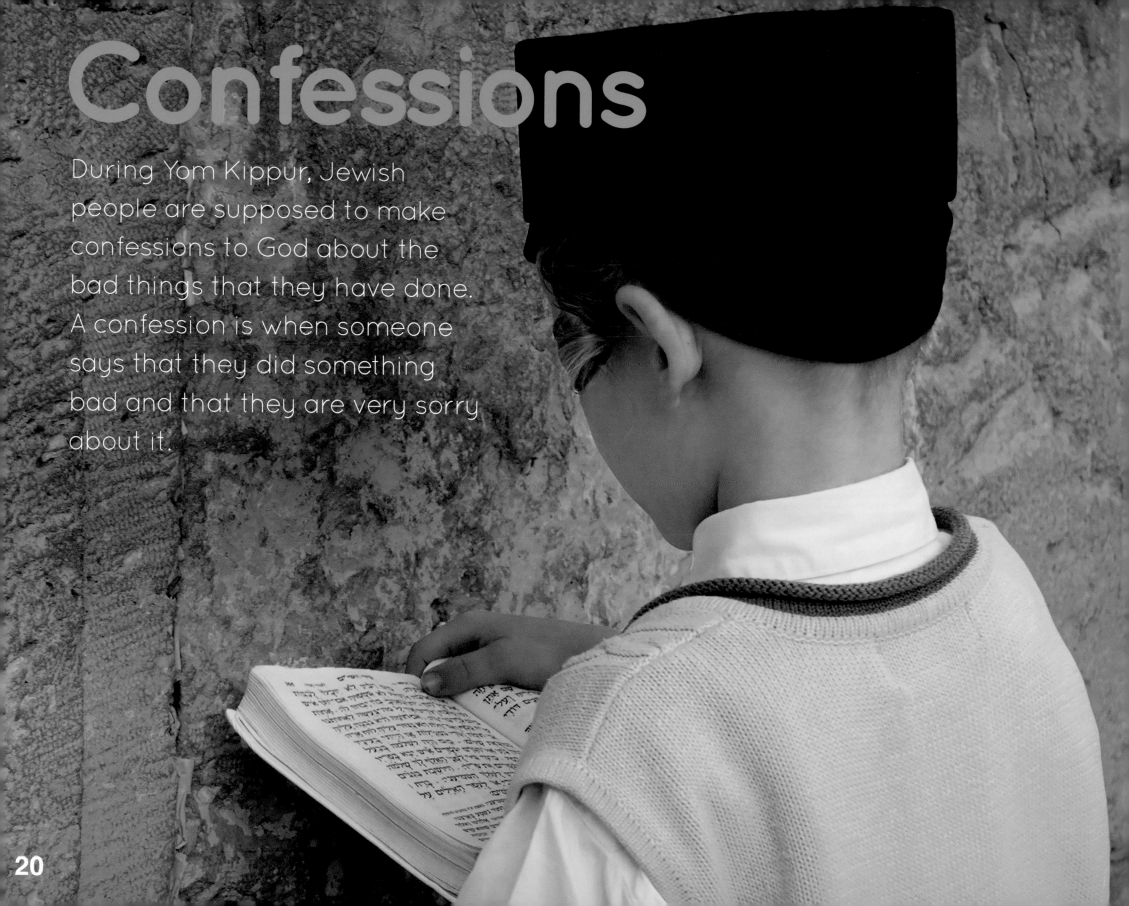

Confessions

During Yom Kippur, Jewish people are supposed to make confessions to God about the bad things that they have done. A confession is when someone says that they did something bad and that they are very sorry about it.

Jewish prayers and confessions are often spoken in Hebrew. Hebrew was the language used by the Israelites and it is still very important in Judaism today.

Jacob says:
VID-OO (Vidui)

Confessions are called 'vidui' in Hebrew.

Jacob Says...

Israelites
Jacob says: IS-RAIL-ITES
A group of Jewish people that lived thousands of years ago.

Kapparot
Jacob says: CAP-PAH-ROT
A way to atone and give to charity during the Yom Kippur festival.

Rabbi
Jacob says: RAB-EYE
A Jewish teacher or leader.

Shofar
Jacob says: SHO-FAR
An instrument that is made from a ram's horn and is used during Jewish festivals.

Synagogue
Jacob says: SIN-A-GOG
A Jewish place of worship.

Vidui
Jacob says: VID-OO
Means 'confession' in Hebrew.

Yamim Noraim
Jacob says: YAM-IM NOR-AIM
A ten-day-long festival when Jewish people
atone for the bad things that they have done.

Yom Kippur
Jacob says: YOM KIP-PER
The most holy day of the year for Jewish people,
also known as the Day of Atonement.

Glossary

atone
make up for the bad things that you have done

charity
a group that tries to help people in need

faith
belief in a religion and a god or gods

religion
a set of beliefs based around a god or gods

slaves
people who are owned by another person and have to do as they say

worship
a religious act where a person shows their love for a god

Index

Credits

Photocredits: Abbreviations: l–left, r–right, b–bottom, t–top, c–centre, m–middle.
Front Cover: bg – Anton_Ivanov; VICTOR TORRES. I – bg – Anton_Ivanov; VICTOR TORRES. 2 – Maglara. 4 – Tom Wang, 5 – Noam Armonn. 6 – Ozgur Guvenc. 7 – Anneka. 8 – Scott Rothstein, 9– Andrey Burmakin. 10 – Matej Kastelic, 11: tr – alexvav; bl – avarand.
12 – Yury Dmitrienko. 13 – ChameleonsEye. 14 – Tomsickova Tatyana. 15 – elbud. 16 – Roman Yanushevsky. 17 – Noam Armonn.
18 – tomertu. 19 – pixelklex. 20 – mikhail. 21 – Konstantin Goldenberg LLC. 22/23 – Marco Govel. Images are courtesy of Shutterstock.com. With thanks to Getty Images, Thinkstock Photo and iStockphoto.